T0145015

GAP

is

Faithtabulous

Eve Cannings

WestBow Press books may be ordered through booksellers or by contacting:

WestBow Press
A Division of Thomas Nelson & Zondervan
1663 Liberty Drive
Bloomington, IN 47403
www.westbowpress.com
1 (866) 928-1240

Because of the dynamic nature of the Internet, any web addresses or links contained
in this book may have changed since publication and may no longer be valid. The views
expressed in this work are solely those of the author and do not necessarily reflect the views
of the publisher, and the publisher hereby disclaims any responsibility for them.

Any people depicted in stock imagery provided by Getty Images are models,
and such images are being used for illustrative purposes only.
Certain stock imagery © Getty Images.

ISBN: 978-1-9736-3994-7 (sc)
ISBN: 978-1-9736-3995-4 (e)

Library of Congress Control Number: 2018910978

Print information available on the last page.

WestBow Press rev. date: 02/22/2019

WESTBOW
PRESS®
A DIVISION OF THOMAS NELSON
& ZONDERVAN

GAP
is
Faithtabulous

"Rise and shine, Everson," Mom said. "Today we are going on a special trip!"

The weather was beautiful!

The sun was shining, the wind was blowing, and the birds were singing.

It was a perfect day for a surprise trip and Everson was excited!

He dressed in a hurry. He tried to imagine where his mom could be taking him on such a beautiful day...

Maybe to a baseball game? Or the ice cream shop?

He could hardly wait to find out what special place they would be visiting!

Everson had so many questions. How long will it take to get there?"

"Are we going to the aquarium?" Everson asked his mom. Mom had promised that one day they would visit the aquarium.

"Pleaseee! Can you give me a clue?"

"Sure!" said Mom.

"We are going to a place where there's a lot to see, and maybe even to touch, BUT you'll have to resist touching anything." The clue sounded more like a rule mom said every time they visited the grocery store, "Look with your eyes, not with your hands."

Everson thought about it some more. Then, he remembered a bible story he had learned!

"Sounds like the garden where Adam and Eve were a long time ago," Everson said. Mom laughed and replied, "Not quite."

"Is it a museum with toy soldiers?" Everson asked. "No." mom replied.

"Is it the grocery store?"

"No, but that's sure a good guess. There's a lot to see and lots of things you'd like to touch, but not today."

"Oh boy," he said. "I guess I'll just have to wait and see."

Mom and Everson rode for a while singing and laughing. They played the game *"I spy."*

They even counted traffic lights. Everson counted ten red lights and mom counted six green lights. Everson was the winner!

Everson peeked out of the window hoping to catch a glimpse of the special place. He remembered the clue his mom gave him…

"Where there was a lot to see and maybe even to touch, but not today."

"I know! I know where we are going!" Everson could see the big sign ahead...PET FRIENDS!

It was the pet store! "Yay!" he shouted. "Maybe today I'll get my beagle," he thought.

Everson had been asking for a beagle for a very long time. He even prayed each night for a beagle. Was this the day that his prayer would be answered?

Everson whispered a prayer, "Dear Jesus, please give me my beagle today."

Finally, they entered the store. Mom gently reminded Everson of her rule, "Look with your eyes, not with your hands." Everson knew exactly what she meant.

They walked each aisle. There was so much to see... birds, fishes, snakes, parrots, cats, bunnies, and then, there were DOGS!

There was a Corgi, a Pug, two Poodles, a Great Dane, a Husky, a Collie, and a pen of puppies.

"Oh, mom, this is the one I prayed for!" Everson said.

He remembered his Bible verse: "Faith is being sure of what we hope for, and certain of what we do not see."

"Mom, can I get him?"

"Sure!" Mom said. "God always rewards obedience. You looked at every animal and never once touched any of them."

"What shall we call him?" Mom asked.

"GAP," Everson replied, because *G*od always *A*nswers *P*rayers.

Everson was happy. It was also just as Mom said "God always hears our prayers and His answers are sometimes yes... no... better... or wait."

Printed in the United States
By Bookmasters